How to Launch a Senseless Argument - or Not!

WILLIAM SEERY, M.Div., M.S., L.M.F.T.

How to Launch a Senseless Argument – Or Not

Web address:
www.pathlightcounseling.com

Email:
northlight4@gmail.com

Edited by Bess Edmunds
Cover design by Bess Edmunds

The concepts presented in *How to Launch a Senseless Argument – or Not!* are generally known and have been gleaned by the author from many years of training and clinical experience in the mental health field. Similarities in the rendering of these principles to other works, if any, are entirely coincidental and non-intentional.

ISBN: 979-8-9888443-2-7

William L Seery, Publisher

Printed in the United States of America

DEDICATION

To my wife, Marcie, for her continual love,
wisdom and support in our every venture.

CONTENTS

PREFACE

For some people, a long book is a chilling instrument of torture, especially a self-help book, aimed at exposing a thousand humiliating faults. However, a short book, one that could make a long-term difference, is worth the risk. *How to Launch a Senseless Argument or Not!* describes the most common damaging yet solvable problem for relationships. A steady pattern of repetitious, senseless arguing ranks first on the Most Damaging list because, with it, other important issues become sealed off from the best solutions. Reversing this pattern opens the best possibilities for healing

I'm happy to make this book available because, for those who are willing to adopt specific suggestions, it will clear the way to address other important issues effectively. Beginner couples can avoid a lot of future trouble; experienced ones can learn to fight a common enemy, instead of each other.

Plus, it *is* short.

Chapter 1

One Year of Marriage, Eight Times

Let's get right to the point. A pattern of regular, repeated arguing will ruin your marriage.

Chuck and Lisa came very close to proving this. After eight years of arguing, the marriage they hoped for was crippled. The deep and rich relationship they had early on had become shallow. Why? Because even in the most committed relationships, persistent arguing eats away at a particular hope and desire built into us all. Fulfilling this desire is one of the primary motives for two individuals to marry. In the beginning, Chuck and Lisa were fully on board with this hope, and they were optimistic. Incidentally, I'm not referring directly to the desire for sex. Then what is it?

Chuck, as a man, and Lisa, as a woman, each longed for a slightly different type of inner assurance and the feeling that comes with it. This male-female difference is common. Of course, not all men or all women would name the exact same desire in focus here. However, from years of clinical experience, plus some limited surveying, I have found a clear consensus about what this desire is for each.

From what I have seen, most men have a deep desire to be competent and for assurance that they truly are competent. Chuck was highly motivated by the hope that he could affect his environment when he set out to design, build, repair, or solve something, to carry out a plan, or to create something that did not exist before. For a man, being capable in these ways is often exhilarating. Generally, a man functions best when he has inner assurance and hope of being personally competent. Adding to that, for most men I have met, the biggest rush comes when he has been competent to please the woman he loves. In the early days of his relationship with Lisa, the assurance and hope of being competent, especially in her eyes, brought out the best in Chuck as a man. Over time, however, when this hope was met with repeated rebuffs from Lisa, the one he loved, it was simply more difficult for him to find courage or stay motivated.

Perhaps some will be concerned that I'm referring only to men loving women, and vice versa. However, the principles I am describing here can be seen in arguments between any two people, including parents and children. I have found it is easiest to illustrate these by showing how they commonly operate in a marriage relationship between a man and a woman. This is because of what I believe are inherent and intended design features we all have.

Additionally, from what I have seen, most women have a deep desire to be personally valued and treasured and to be reassured that they are truly treasured. Lisa agreed with this one hundred percent. Yet for a long while, she did not see evidence of that assurance from Chuck. Of course, everyone wants to be valued, and possibly everyone would like to be seen as competent. However, if we go with the notion that this desire for being valued is generally more intently sought after by women, it will help to see how the lack of assurance of value feeds into a pattern of arguing.

Once, I traveled with a group of friends to the city of Venice, Italy. In one of the shops there, I saw a beautiful, hand-crafted jewelry box. A true work of art, it reflected the mystique of Venice, plus it reminded me of a friend back home who was a master artist. *"Angie would love this,"* I thought. So, I bought it for her.

Back home, when my friend received the gift, wrapped carefully and brought halfway around the world, from the city of love, it had a much greater impact on her than I intended. If you can imagine what that impact was, you are more astute than I was when I purchased it. For her, it carried almost the same message as an engagement ring! Oops.

Naively, I underestimated how powerful this symbol would be for this young woman. A beautiful jewelry box signals the presence of something much more valuable being protected inside. For her, it embodied her deep, legitimate, natural longing to be valued. When a woman possesses a high degree of assurance of her personal value, it is easier for her to offer her best and most loving self.

So, how was this situation with Angie resolved? It was awkward and hurtful, especially for her. However, she was very mature and handled it with grace.

Now, what if a man doubts that he is competent or that he is seen as such? And, what if a woman sees no evidence that she is valued by the man she loves?

Right or wrong, the most common response for a male when his hope of competence is threatened is first to disconnect emotionally. Second, he instinctively shifts his focus to a venue where he can find the feeling of being competent. He may go to work or to his workshop to create or fix something. He may even head to the wilderness. This is what Chuck did, frequently. It was quiet there, and no one complained about his faults — faults which he was much too aware of already. At least in the wild was the prospect of being competent to bring back a trophy for his efforts. Perhaps the most common and easy refuge is pornography, or even the real embrace of another woman. For these venues in particular, a man's sense of competence is not challenged until the hypnotic mood is broken and he realizes the profound damage he has done by violating his primary loyalty.

The most common female response when her hope of being valued is threatened is, first, to try reestablishing the empathic connection with him. Often, with a sense of urgency or even panic, she attempts this by using verbal reasoning and proofs. In the process, she draws from a very large database—mental records of exact times, places, tones of voice, topics, and circumstances. Most often, these records are accurate and precise. To Lisa, her sense of emotional connection was vital. When she could not sense it, she went into reconnection mode big time. Mentally, she consulted her extensive inner database and put together an airtight verbal case against Chuck that he could never refute. Historically, humankind has greatly benefited from women who are excellent researchers and scientists, using data for great outcomes. But why would someone keep and remember details like these? In Lisa's case, it was to answer an extremely important question: "Can I trust that I am truly valued by this person I love?"

Arguments and Rocket Science

Now, let's talk about rockets. Better, let's talk about how arguments are like rockets. To fly a rocket or an argument, there must be fuel, and since a rocket has a purpose, there is some kind of payload, something it carries related to fulfilling its purpose. This is the part that draws the most attention. Usually, this purpose is either about people, like astronauts, or explosives which make a lot of noise and have spectacular effects. The payload of a rocket almost always sits on the very top.

An argument also carries what seems to be a purpose, or payload, and this is the part that gets the most attention, like fireworks. While this *appears* to be the most important part of the argument, especially to the people arguing, in fact, it is not. The most rational-sounding part of the argument is the *topic*. It's on the top. Get it, the 'top-ic'?

Two types of fuel, when combined, drive the argument/rocket into the sky. One type of fuel is the man, who wishes —or even covets— to be competent enough to please the woman; and the woman, who wishes to be valued by the man. What does it take to ignite the argument? It could be a tone of voice, or a repeat offense, an attempt to address a problem, or who knows, maybe even a spiritual influence.

Whatever sparks it, the launch is a "go." The argument rises, slow at first, then faster and louder, spewing flames, smoke, animus, hurt, and anger upward into the open sky. Some flights or fights last for hours, while others are short. Either way, when the fuel runs out, or either partner literally runs out, the argument falls back to earth.

Each unproductive argument damages each person a little more and progressively drains them of courage. Consequently, with every argument, each person is a little more dis-couraged. After many, many of these hope-depleting episodes, something ominous begins to happen in three stages. Looking back, Chuck and Lisa could see that their relationship had been deteriorating in this progression.

First Stage

Over time, they were losing compassion, passion, and even interest in each other. Whenever they came together, they only expected the worst. For instance, after a long day's sincere effort at work or home, Chuck braced himself, knowing he would hear more from his wife about how he is failing as a husband or father. Meanwhile, Lisa was despairing of her hope that Chuck would ever be motivated to change. Nearly every evening, their interactions consisted of either loud debates or subtle, mutual, discounting jabs. Looking back, they could say that their eight-year marriage felt more like one year repeated eight times, and they were both tired.

Second Stage

In stage two, a great mountain was taking shape. Each bickering, shaming argument layered itself onto the last one and the next one after that, until a hill was formed. Layers of resentment caused the hill to rise and grow larger, turning into despair. Chuck found it hard to even pretend everything was okay in social gatherings. Lisa became sarcastic. Their argument pattern had grown to be a mountain. It became Mount Olympus. A great cloud formed around it. Lightning bolts were being thrown by mythical gods within each of them because they were each forming their own mythology! This mythology was the story they told themselves about each other. Desperately, they were each groping for a way to account for the pain they were experiencing.

"It must be him because I know how hard I try to make it work," thought Lisa.

"It must be her because I know how hard I try to make it work," complained Chuck to himself.

Depressing, huh? Keep going, though, because even though things got worse, there was a way forward.

Third Stage

Stage three is like the third stage of a rocket (rockets again!) where the original cause of the problem falls away from everyone's focus. It happens a lot. In this phase, one or both people reach out for help. A friend, a counselor, a pastor, or rabbi all give their advice. Internet sites and advice blogs bring opinions from a lot of different angles. And there are books. Most compelling are the ones that talk all about what it is like to be married to a narcissist.

"That explains everything. I'm married to a narcissist! He (or she) fits eight out of the ten signs."

In this case, the mythology validates the idea that the spouse has a formal psychological character disorder, and even more comforting, at least at first, a convenient label to go with it.

It could be true. He or she could truly have a true personality disorder! It *does* happen. However, since this notion has become part of the growing mythology, and many of the symptoms come from their shared history, we can't determine if someone really fits the diagnosis until we get out of that cloud! The cloud *fogs* the issue, so to speak. The problem with all the help offered to this couple is that everyone is weighing in *on the cloud*, the mythology, the story being told to explain all that pain and resentment. The helpers are focusing on that mythology and even the topics of arguments, rather than the pattern of arguing that has been making the couple sick.

Lisa's friends sympathized. Some of them empathized. Her pastor truly cared and suggested that she work on being more submissive. "Miraculously, it worked for my wife," he said. Lisa's therapist, after five individual sessions with Lisa (none with

Chuck), diagnosed Lisa with depression and Chuck with a personality disorder to keep himself from feeling inadequate as a professional. He recommended a book for Lisa that gave her a new clarity about what was wrong with Chuck. At first, the feeling of relief it brought to Lisa was like a glorious sunrise after a cold night. The notion that he had a personality disorder explained everything she was experiencing. Finally, it seemed to make sense.

"*If only Chuck were like my therapist!*" she said, only to herself.

Not long after this glint of relief, the scorching heat of day set in as she felt she now needed to do something. But what?

Chuck had only one close friend: his name was Doug. When Chuck shared his situation with him, Doug said, "Yeah, me too", and "Hey, I got drawn for that elk tag, want to go with me next week?"

So, what is the leading cause of divorce? Maybe the answer to that question calls for a little rocket science. It is a pattern of repeated, escalating arguments, fueled by mutual discounting and discouragement. To make a real difference, we must start with the cause and shift it into reverse.

How to Reverse and Replace the Argument Pattern

Many couples are in a tailspin because of the destructive scenario we have just described. Is there a way to pull out of it? Can their relationship be salvaged? Yes. It can become deeper and stronger and better than ever.

By following these four steps, Chuck and Lisa were able to sabotage the launch of senseless arguments, reverse their destructive and discouraging pattern, and replace it with one that works.

Use Off-Time for Mutual Encouragement

"Off-time" refers to when no argument or conflict is happening. Use these hours (or even minutes) well because the first goal for each person is to establish and reinforce a new pattern of building the other person up. Don't worry about getting a good response for now or having instant results. Make it a gift to the other person, for free. Conventional wisdom does not usually direct us to build up and strengthen our enemy. However, the other person is *not* your enemy, though he or she may be acting like one. Furthermore, we tend to act from weakness or discouragement when we are immersed in a negative argument pattern, so you want the other person to be strong, not weak. It is a lot easier to move to the next step when both parties have encouragement.

Incidentally, some couples play out this "argument" scenario quietly. They rarely get into the loud escalation of an obvious verbal battle. Instead, they drain and deplete each other with silence at just the right time, or by precision bombing with criticism at just the right target. Sarcasm is often used in this way. Whether quiet or loud, it is discouraging for both, and a solution is needed.

Real solutions must be based on an understanding of what makes a problem work. A couple can love each other, be committed, well-motivated, loving to their kids, knowledgeable, yet still be at each other's throats. Chuck and Lisa were all of these things. Married for eight years, they were committed, loved their kids, had steady jobs, *and* were at each other's throats.

After countless skirmishes, Chuck became certain that Lisa saw him as inept and incompetent, especially incompetent to please her. Lisa was convinced that, on a scale from one to ten, Chuck valued her as little as 'one.' And she believed it was that high because of all the housework she did, plus occasional sex. She had gathered a lot of evidence to support what she thought was wrong with Chuck and used it whenever she could to prove her point. She did it, hoping sincerely that he would finally "get it" and change. She was exhausted.

Lisa did not know whether Chuck would implement step one. However, she realized she did not need his permission or an agreement from him. She did not need him to do his part for her to do her part. So, she started by looking for ways to affirm his competence. She took seriously the idea that Chuck, as a man, might find encouragement and strength from seeing that he was competent in her eyes. Whenever she saw him do *anything* well or when he did anything that pleased her, she was determined not to hide her pleasure. She found some direct and effective ways to express this, such as a smile, a "thank you," or "I really liked it when you…." She made compliments simple and brief. It seemed to hit home the most when she described her experience of a particular positive action on his part and what it did for her. "Hey, it helped me a lot when you took the kids out to play. Thanks," and "Today I was thinking about how much energy you put into providing for us, and I felt grateful."

Chuck also decided he would do his part without trying to get her to do hers. Really, he did not think she would do it anyway. So, he thought about the good things she brought to his life, aside from the trouble they were having as a couple. He tried to think of what made her feel important and valued in the past. He remembered the times—eons ago it seemed—that she had written him cards, and the night she brought him a blanket when he was sitting outside, and it was getting cold. He started to plan and design things he could do that she would most easily interpret as him valuing her. His first attempts were awkward, though. For example, one night he made dinner to surprise her. While the chicken was on the grill, he went on YouTube "for just a second" to look up how to change the fuel pump in his truck and forgot all about the chicken. When Chuck finally put out the grill fire, that started in his absence, Lisa couldn't tell that it was chicken and accused him of mocking her by making charcoal for dinner. That launched a big argument with lots of fireworks. She went out for tacos by herself that night.

However, Chuck was not one to give up. He took that incident as a practice run. Over the next few weeks, he made other attempts with more success. Lisa noticed his effort, and it felt good. The effort was more important to her than his level of expertise.

Shut Down the Countdown

In a final launch countdown, suspense rises toward the moment of liftoff: we know when the launch is scheduled, yet it could be scrubbed at any point. In an argument, we may not have ten seconds before we realize it is launching, but shutting it down early is a good idea.

Conditions leading up to the onset of an argument often go unnoticed by either person, even as the tension rises. Fatigue after a long day, low blood sugar before dinner, and many other factors all add fuel to the launch. However, sometimes we can see it coming. Chuck saw it coming when he had to tell Lisa he canceled their date night without consulting her because his high school friend was in town. Lisa saw it coming when she signed them both up to run the snack bar at their kids' soccer game on a Friday night. It is good to be ready for the triggers if you can or at least know what to look for. In other words, rather than counting down to liftoff, we should look for the smoke and roar signaling that an argument is igniting.

Most people don't like to argue, and they rarely start an argument on purpose. Some people may find this hard to believe. However, most conflicts really are triggered unexpectedly: a certain topic, tone of voice, an offensive comment, or an insinuation of guilt. Ideally, we would want to shut down or sabotage the argument, then flip it into a real conversation. To do this well, first consider what happens in real time when two people argue, no matter what the topic:

- Speech gets louder and faster. Tone of voice gets higher.
- Voices are more rhythmic and melodic back and forth.
- Breathing becomes rapid and shallower.
- CO2 levels in the blood increase.
- Adrenaline increases.
- Anxiety increases.

- Posture is more animated and threatening, usually standing.
- Physical gestures become more frequent and larger.
- Both become *extremely compulsive*, yet each believes he is being rational.
- The "conversation" is replaced by a debate. The goal of a debate is to *WIN*!

With all these things happening, how can we possibly get even one of these negative interactions to reverse direction? With most arguments, both parties inadvertently add fuel to keep it going. Consequently, it falls on the first person who notices one or more of the symptoms mentioned above to begin the shutdown procedure. There is no need to wait until the other person also realizes it. The goal is to control only yourself, not the other person.

So, there is a "shutdown procedure?" Yes. It begins when, individually, we implement one or more specific behaviors when the conflict begins to escalate. Chapter 2 offers a list of suggested behaviors to try. Look it over, pick a few of these suggestions to memorize and practice. Shutting down senseless arguments consistently takes practice.

Again, it is not enough to know about these behavior changes or to try only once. For example, when Chuck learned that it was possible to shut down senseless arguments, he began experimenting because he was sick of them. He became familiar with a few of the suggestions listed in Chapters 2 and 3.

For starters, Chuck began noticing when any of their conversations morphed into a back-and-forth debate. Compulsively, he and Lisa would start opposing each other verbally without really listening to what the other was saying. Chuck learned to treat this "debate mode" as his signal to show interest and respect for what Lisa had just said, no matter how much he disagreed. He began to accept what she was saying as *her* expression of what *she* thinks, rather than something that he had to disprove. Whenever he did that, it gave Lisa a little more *experience* of being taken seriously, which is what she wanted more than she wanted to be right.

For instance, on one occasion, Lisa alleged, "You think you can spend money on whatever you want. You don't even care enough to tell me."

Immediately, Chuck thought of a time when he had consulted with her before buying something, even though it was over a year ago. He was ready to fire back to prove her wrong when he suddenly remembered his plan. For him, it was like when the check engine light came on in his car. But in this case, the warning light said, "stupid debate."

"Hey, would you say that again?" he said. Then, "So, is that what it looks like to you? Could you tell me more about that? I really do want to know."

At first, Lisa did not trust that he really did "really did want to know". However, the more he showed interest in what she said and *her* perspective without debating it, the easier it was for her to let down her guard. She became less accusatory. He became more motivated to try to understand her. This was the opposite of arguing.

Chuck had some success with another approach to shutting down an argument. When he noticed that their voices were getting louder and faster, he took charge of his own voice and slowed it down a bit. He also turned the volume down on purpose. This was not for dramatic effect, but for de-escalating tensions. It helped.

Did Chuck and Lisa ever have a senseless argument again? Yep! However, it happened much less often because each argument would tend to fizzle out before it got off the launch pad. Other times, however, they just skipped over the shutdown procedure completely. The argument rocket would get so high that it would be in orbit. The old pattern was back?! What now?

Drop Out of Orbit, Slowly

Chuck and Lisa loved each other. Still, the times they escalated their disagreements compulsively to a very high altitude were too frequent. Chuck called them "mad dog" arguments because their determination to win felt so insane. At that altitude and with that intensity, not only were the conflicts mutually discouraging, but they were damaging as well. With every argument, the mountain of distortion and resentment grew.

The word "love" is often used as a verb, and it should be when dropping out of orbit. This couple took positive action on their negative pattern. Like before, they had to start adopting a few new behaviors to implement during intense interactions with each other. One of these had to do with breathing.

In orbit, there is no oxygen. You must bring your own. Underwater, it's the same way. Without enough oxygen, panic can set in easily, so breathing must be deliberate. Similarly, our breathing changes when an argument gets intense. Often, we feel the effects throughout our body, and it produces a compulsive feeling. Like gasping for air, the compulsion to refute the other person's last statement can take over. Whether it is in outer space, underwater, or in the middle of an argument, when we feel out of control, our first and best point of leverage is to control our breathing. Incidentally, one of the first rules of SCUBA diving is, "Don't panic, take control of your breathing."

Lisa grasped this principle first, during a conflict. She thought of a perfect rebuttal to Chuck's excuse for locking his keys in his car — again. Poised and ready to fire back at him, it suddenly dawned on her that she was far more interested in making her point and correcting him than she should have been. Plus, she felt a little lightheaded. Lisa purposely took a very deep breath, deeper than was comfortable. Then, she let her breath out very slowly, yet without making it obvious. By doing this, she missed her "turn" in their debate, listened twice as long to his comments without refuting what he said, and she felt an odd sense of relief. Next, she slowed her breathing down and relaxed her posture. Instead of trying to control Chuck, she was consciously managing and taking control of herself. By doing this, she was able to "drop out of orbit" in the argument without discounting him or disconnecting. When she did this, she usually found that Chuck would follow suit.

Breathing is an example of how physiology can be involved in a conflict. Lisa found a few other ways to de-escalate an argument in progress. For instance, she would listen for anything Chuck said that she could agree with, then affirm it back to him with conviction.

One conflict had been going on for ten minutes or so. Chuck said to her, "Your precious cell phone is like a drug to you!"

Angered at first, then realizing there was a certain amount of truth to his comment, she said, "Oh my gosh, I can't believe you said that! I think you are right. I *am* hooked on it. Yesterday I figured out that I spent five hours looking at it. Why? Most of what I watched was meaningless."

Chuck was expecting her to debate his point but didn't know how to respond to her agreeing with him. The conflict began to de-escalate. He eventually shared that he also feels the same automatic compulsion to grab his phone. This was something they could unite over. They decided to look for ways to replace time on the phone with time together.

Lisa and Chuck made good use of another insight. Chuck had a close friend named Scott who shared something he learned about the word "sarcasm" as it is in Greek. "Sarc" means "flesh," and "casm" means "to cut." Sarcasm hurts. It also carries a built-in plausible deniability. For instance, using a slightly derogatory tone, Chuck would say to Lisa in front of friends, "Lisa *loves* to cook for big groups. Don't you Lisa?" He knew that Lisa hated cooking for big groups. Chuck's statement could have been taken two ways, but they both knew it was meant to be critical of her and embarrassing.

Few people who are trapped in the argument pattern described here are able to reverse it instantly. With practice, the pattern can change. But what about times when we forget all these suggestions or they "just don't seem to work," especially when an episode seems to be a complete blowout?

Debrief the Argument

Stay on track and redeem conflicts that do not go well by making a mutual commitment in advance to debrief the arguments. Some will read this and think the idea is to debrief the *topic*. No, not the topic, *the argument.*

Chuck and Lisa did this. Here is how it looked: Thirty minutes after an unhinged, high-altitude argument about who had left the gate open when their dog ran away, Chuck had cooled off enough to initiate a conversation.

"Hey, I want to take a few minutes and go over our disagreement. Are you able to do that?"

Lisa really did not want to, partly because she feared it would rekindle the conflict. But she reminded herself that the purpose was to address the way they disagreed rather than to address the topic, which they did not see the same way. She agreed, and they met at the kitchen table.

Chuck started. "Ok, so what was that argument like for you?"

"I felt humiliated and blamed when I didn't deserve it," said Lisa.

"I guess that explains why you did what you did," he replied.

Lisa flared a little. "You mean when I threw my cell phone at your truck, I guess. What went through your mind when I did that?"

"I was pretty surprised by it. Plus, I was worried that maybe I pushed you over the edge or something. I don't really want to be that guy," said Chuck.

"Actually, I'm glad to hear that. I just thought I didn't matter to you at all," she said.

"That's not at all how I feel toward you, but I was mad. Sorry you felt that way. I'll work on making it clearer that I love you and I care about how you feel. Let's see if we can talk it out next time." Then Chuck, risking a joke, said: "Besides, we can't afford more cell phones."

Together you can work through nearly any topic, but senseless arguments, especially a pattern of arguing, are your real common enemy. It is also the enemy of your marriage and the family you have been working hard to build. The same is true for conflicts in a parent-child relationship.

So far, we have talked about how arguments work and how they build up a mountain of negative history in the relationship that too easily determines the future. For those who are willing to act on it, we have also suggested a systematic way to reverse this argument pattern. To speed up positive change in your relationship, I suggest going back over what was presented here. Highlight or make notes on any parts of it that may apply to your situation. Then practice applying it in your real-time interactions. Be experimental. Don't stop at one attempt. Some find it helpful to memorize certain insights or ways to phrase relevant things. The next two chapters contain a collection of insights about hurtful tactics commonly used in senseless arguments and suggestions for finding the right words to build each other up instead.

Chapter 2

Twelve Hurtful Argument Tactics and How to Reverse Them

Check the boxes and circles below that best describe what you tend to do.

1. **Using words and actions that threaten each other's hope that their deepest desire (such as being valued or seen as competent) will ever be fulfilled.**

   LOOKS LIKE

   ☐ Chuck: "I don't have to tell you about every penny I spend."

   ☐ Lisa: "You don't get what it takes to manage anything, much less money!"

   TRY THIS

- Chuck: "Lisa, you are always welcome to know about the money I spend."

- Lisa: "I know you could manage anything, including money. It just makes me feel more important to you when we discuss decisions together."

2. **Body language and verbal responses demonstrate that you are not listening or interested in what the other person is saying.**

LOOKS LIKE

- ☐ Chuck turns and walks away when she brings up her concern and says, "Here we go again!"

- ☐ Lisa interrupts him. "Here *YOU* go again!"

TRY THIS

- Chuck: When Lisa brings up her concern, Chuck starts to turn and walk away, then realizes it will be seen as an insult, so he comes back and sits down with Lisa. He says, "I see this is important to you, so ok, let's talk."

- Lisa says, "I know you may not want to talk about this, but it means a lot to me, so please stop and discuss it with me."

3. **Most expressions and statements are negative, condemning, disrespectful, or disqualifying.**

LOOKS LIKE

- ☐ Lisa: "You know what I expect? I expect you to minimize this and run away."
- ☐ Chuck: "Yeah, well, I expect you to expect the worst."

TRY THIS

- ○ Lisa: "You know what I expect? I expect that even if you struggle with this, you will overcome it."
- ○ Chuck: "Yeah, well, sometimes I expect rejection from you, but then you show me a lot of grace. Thank you."

4. **Statements are dogmatic and authoritative and make no exceptions.**

LOOKS LIKE

- ☐ Lisa: "You think you can spend whatever you want. You don't care about what I think."
- ☐ Chuck: "I already know what you think."

TRY THIS

- ○ Lisa: "I'm pretty sure you think differently about money than I do, but I think we can still come to an agreement about it.

- ○ Chuck: "I guess I don't really know what you are thinking."

5. **Sarcasm ("Sarc"= flesh, and "casm" = to cut) and tone of voice are condemning, as if to say "stupid".**

LOOKS LIKE

- ☐ Lisa: "That's great, now you can read people's minds. You are soooo smart!"
- ☐ Chuck: "Not as smart as YOU, Miss Know Everything."

TRY THIS

- ○ Chuck: "I wish you could read my mind. You might be pleasantly surprised. You really are smart, though."
- ○ Chuck: "Thanks, Lisa. I'm glad you think so."

6. **Neither person gives the other credit for anything positive unless it is to set them up for criticism and shaming.**

LOOKS LIKE

- ☐ Lisa: "I take it back; you really are smart. Then why can't you understand the simplest math?"

☐ Chuck: "You got straight As in school, but not in keeping track of money."

TRY THIS

○ Lisa: "I'm pretty sure you think differently about money than I do, but I think we can still come to an agreement about it."

○ Chuck: "I guess I shouldn't assume what you are thinking."

7. Each person tells the other all about their thoughts and motives as if they were a mind-reader.

LOOKS LIKE

☐ Lisa: "You have no idea what I go through. You don't even think of me all day."

☐ Chuck: "If you really cared, you wouldn't just complain all the time."

TRY THIS

○ Lisa: "I do want you to understand what I go through. I may be wrong, but I wonder if you think of me all day."

○ Chuck: "I do, a lot, but when you list a lot of complaints in a row, I shut down."

8. **Each person blurts out authoritative judgments about a topic or situation without respect for feelings.**

LOOKS LIKE

☐ Lisa: "You're like all the other deadbeat men I've ever met."

☐ Chuck: "You only married me for money and to impress people."

TRY THIS

○ Lisa: "I'm glad you are not like a lot of men out there."

○ Chuck: "The world absolutely needs more women like you."

9. **Each person matches the other's last statement with a symmetrical, but more intense response.**

LOOKS LIKE

☐ Lisa: "Even Jerry commented that all you do is wander around at work talking to people."

☐ Chuck: "Well, Jerry's wife told me that all *you* do is criticize me behind my back."

☐ Lisa: "Who criticized who behind whose back?"

☐ Chuck: "You criticize you-know-who behind MY back."

TRY THIS

○ Lisa: "Even Jerry commented that you encourage everyone at work."

○ Chuck: "Jerry's wife told me that you compliment me even when I'm not there."

10. Each person interrupts the other, often not letting them finish statements.

LOOKS LIKE

☐ Lisa: "What do you mean, you are the one who..."

☐ Chuck: "No, it's you, you are the one who . . ."

☐ Lisa: "Me? Not me, it's you."

TRY THIS

○ Lisa: "But you said . . ., It's okay, you go ahead. Finish what you were saying."

○ Chuck: "No, you, you are the one who... wait, sorry, I interrupted you. "

11. Each person portrays themselves as either absolutely justified or as the victim of the other person's actions.

LOOKS LIKE

☐ Chuck: "I can't even do my job because of you."

☐ Lisa: "I do more for you than anyone, without fail, but you don't appreciate it."

TRY THIS

○ Chuck: "Sometimes you frustrate me so much I want to scream, but I know you don't mean to."

○ Lisa: "I forget how much you do for me; overall, I do appreciate it."

12. **Both describe situations or actions using absolute terms like: "always," "every time," "never," "none," "completely," and "not once have you ever…."**

LOOKS LIKE

☐ Chuck: "Never once have you said, 'I'm sorry.'"

☐ Lisa: "Well, you always talk over me, and I never, ever get a chance to talk."

TRY THIS

○ Chuck: "I know you did apologize, so thanks for that."

- O Lisa: "It's not like you always interrupt me, but when you do, I feel very discounted by you".

What I Intend to Put into Practice

Number of Boxes I Checked (hurtful tactics)	Number of Circles I Checked (constructive)
Suggestions I Want to Keep and Use	

Chapter 3

Tips for Reducing Senseless Arguments

Here are some specific suggestions for how to cut back on the duration and frequency of arguments. Highlight or circle any of them you decide to practice. Then write these in on the space provided at the end of the list. Always find a way to capture any valuable idea before it slips away. Life is busy.

How to "Use Off-Time for Mutual Encouragement"

- Express gratefulness *very* frequently for things the other person does.
- Replace negative comments with positive (and true) ones, like:
  "This could be a good game." vs "Why go, we'll probably lose anyway."

- Initiate and protect time together, like planning a date.
- Anticipate chores the other person intends to do for that day and do them yourself.
- Assume the best motives rather than the worst, even when it may not seem that way. Avoid judging.
- Do surprise, out-of-context favors and expressions of value, like a card, a compliment, or folding clothes.
- Call each other by name and with a positive tone of voice. Arguing couples seem to forget each other's names.

How to "Shut Down the Countdown"

- Do not use sarcasm or let your tone of voice be condemning, as if to say, "STUPID!"
- Preface what you say by giving the other person credit for something positive (and true).
- Say, "Tell me more," and "What else," rather than you continuing to talk.
- Before you speak, try to anticipate how your words might be taken the wrong way, then rephrase them for clarity.
- Pray for wisdom and follow it.
- Clarify what it is you are *not* saying when you see how you may be misinterpreted.
- Give each other credit for *anything* you can think of, as long as it is true.

How to "Drop Out of Orbit"

- Interrupt the natural rhythm of the argument, take one big breath, and let it out very slowly (not dramatically!).
- Relax physically. Get comfortable, breathe slowly.
- Speak slower, not faster.
- Speak for and about *yourself* rather than as an expert on the other person.
- Let the other person know what you hear and ask him or her if you are correct.
- Look for ways to compliment the other person rather than shaming or proving them wrong.

How To "Debrief" after an Argument

- Apologize for *any* part of it that was your fault. Be specific. Ask for forgiveness.
- Forgive each other, but allow time for the emotions to catch up with you and with the other person.
- Plan together for what you will do at the onset of the next argument, to turn it into a conversation rather than a debate.

What I Intend to Put into Practice

Chapter 4

Senseless or Sensible? You Decide

A Senseless Version

Normal, everyday interactions can include occasional negative or even offensive comments without these being deal-breakers for the relationship. However, when they creep into and pervade our communication with each other, it is *truly* toxic. Without focusing on the topic, notice what it must feel like for Chuck or Lisa hearing rapid-fire negative comments like the ones below. Even when these samples may not fully characterize one conversation, they still retain their damaging effect when they are spread over many interactions.

Chuck: "I don't have to tell you about every penny I spend."

Lisa: "You don't get what it takes to manage anything, much less money!"

Chuck: Turns and walks away when Lisa brings up her

concern and says, "Here we go again!"

Lisa: Interrupts him. "Here YOU go again!"

Lisa: "You know what I expect? I expect you to minimize this and run away."

Chuck: "Yeah, well, I expect you to expect the worst."

Lisa: "You think you can spend whatever you want. You don't care about what I think."

Chuck: "I already know what you think."

Lisa: "That's great, now you can read people's minds. You are soooo smart!"

Chuck: "Not as smart as YOU, Miss Know Everything."

Lisa: "I take it back. You really are smart. So why can't you understand the simplest math?"

Chuck: "You got straight As in school, but not in keeping track of money."

Lisa: "You have no idea what I go through. You don't even think of me all day."

Chuck: "If you really cared, you wouldn't just complain all the time."

Lisa: "You're like all the other deadbeat men I've ever met."

Chuck: "You only married me for my money and to impress people."

Lisa: "Even Jerry commented that all you do is wander around at work talking to people."

Chuck: "Well, Jerry's wife told me that all you do is criticize me behind my back."

Lisa: "Who criticized who behind whose back?"

Chuck: "You criticize you-know-who behind MY back."

Lisa: "What do you mean, you are the one who . . ."

Chuck: "No, you, you are the one who . . . "

Lisa: "Me? Not me, it's you."

Chuck: "I don't know how much more of this I can take."

Lisa: "I do more for you than anyone, without fail, but you don't appreciate it."

Chuck: "Never once have you ever said, "I'm sorry."

Lisa: "Well, you always talk over me and I never, ever get a chance to talk."

Chuck: "I don't even want to go home."

Lisa: "I don't have any feelings. I just want to quit."

Of course, if every comment we make to each other is only positive and overly nice, it might be no different than a recipe for syrup, or sarcasm! Nevertheless, look at the more constructive alternatives to defensive responses below. What if expressions like these permeated our interactions, yet in a more natural way? It would be a good first step to mitigate senseless conflict. Plus, it would not be toxic.

A More Sensible Version

Chuck: "Lisa, you are always welcome to know about all the money I spend."

Lisa: "I know you could manage anything, including money. Please use your ability more with us in mind. It will make me feel more like I am important to you."

Chuck: (When she brings up her concern, Chuck starts to turn and walk away, then realizes it will be seen as an insult, so he comes back and sits down with Lisa. Then he says, "I see this is important to you, so ok, let's talk."

Lisa: "I know you may not want to talk about this, but it means a lot to me, so please stop and discuss it with me."

Lisa: "You know what I expect? I expect that even if you struggle with this, you will overcome it."

Chuck: "Yeah, well, sometimes I expect rejection from you, but then you show me a lot of grace. Thank you."

Lisa: "I'm pretty sure you think differently about money than I do, but I think we can still come to an agreement about it.

Chuck: "I guess I don't really know what you are thinking."

Lisa: "I wish you could read my mind. You might be pleasantly surprised. You really are smart, though."

Chuck: "Not as smart as you."

Lisa: "I think we are both smart enough to solve this together."

Chuck: "Either way, you are better at keeping track of money than I am."

Lisa: "I do want you to understand what I go through. I may be wrong, but I wonder if you think of me all day."

Chuck: "I do, a lot, but when you list a lot of complaints in a row, I shut down.

Lisa: "I'm glad you are not like a lot of men out there."

Chuck: "You only married me for money and to impress people." (Meant as a joke, and they both laugh.)

Lisa: "Even Jerry commented that you encourage everyone at work."

Chuck: "Well, Jerry's wife told me that you compliment me even when I'm not there."

Lisa: "Who compliments whom behind whose back?"

Chuck: "Seems like everyone compliments you behind your back." (Both laugh)

Lisa: "What do you mean, you are the one who..."

Chuck: "No, you, you are the one who... wait, sorry, I interrupted you. "

Lisa: "It's ok, you go ahead. Finish what you were saying."

Chuck: "Sometimes you frustrate me so much I want to scream, but I know you don't mean to."

Lisa: "I forget how much you do for me, but overall, I do appreciate it."

Chuck: "I know you did apologize, so thanks for that."

Lisa: "If you talk over me, it makes me tune you out, so please wait till I'm done talking. Thank you."

Chuck: "I long for the time when we could automatically encourage each other. I even looked forward to coming home. I know we can get that back."

Lisa: "I am discouraged but definitely do not want to quit."

What I Intend to Put into Practice

Chapter 5

Conclusion

Make it Safe Enough to Go Deeper

Chuck and Lisa had a floundering marriage, and yes, they did save it. But what if they had deeper issues than their argument pattern? Well . . . they did. Big issues.

With practice, they replaced their bickering style of not really communicating with healthy communicating. Being together became more mutually encouraging and safer. They were picking up where they had left off early in the relationship, when they were getting to know each other. A new process of discovery was underway.

Eventually, though, Chuck and Lisa discovered things about each other that were alarming and even hurtful, things they had not known or realized. For instance, Lisa learned that in his teen years, Chuck had gotten into the habit of visiting porn sites. When he finally realized how damaging this was to himself and to having a close, honest relationship, he decided to stop. He really meant it. However, he found that stopping was more difficult than he expected. Along with that, the pattern of arguing in his marriage with Lisa had made it more tempting to check out in this way, and it blocked them from talking about it productively. Was it her fault? Nope. Porn was his issue; however, it was made worse by their divide-and-conquer arguing pattern before it was addressed.

Chuck also discovered some things about Lisa. As they became better at listening to and learning about each other on deeper levels, she began sharing things from her past she had never mentioned before. She had considered many of these experiences as "water under the bridge." Some of what lay beneath that bridge caused emotional injuries. Sexual trauma was a big part of it, and the effects had made their way into her adult life and marriage. For her, some of these effects frequently appeared in the form of being especially mean and critical.

So, for Chuck and Lisa, arguing might not seem to have been the biggest problem after all. But in fact, it was. All those senseless arguments had been effectively sealing them off from each other, like bugs encased in plastic for sale at a highway truck stop. The healing potential that was built into the basic design of marriage had been frozen in place.

With the obstacle of senseless arguing out of the way, Chuck and Lisa were more able and motivated to unite over their deeper issues. For them, a therapist was very useful in helping them sort things out in a way that made them stronger. It was difficult, but worth it.

Best-case Marriage?

What would an ideal marriage look like? If we did an opinion survey, no doubt people would describe a marriage that is completely free of conflict, both people always positive, lots of sex, plenty of money, admiring friends. However, from what I have seen, the best marriages have the following four characteristics in this order of priority.

First, the couple functions in a way that is consistent with their original design. Chuck and Lisa believed they were each purposely designed by God to be different in ways that are complementary, like colors that match, for mutual love. They functioned best when they aligned themselves with this design by honoring it, and worse when they spent their energy defending themselves against each other.

Second, in the best marriages, both parties together generate more than they both could individually. This is usually referred to as synergy. With obstacles out of the way, Chuck and Lisa were able to experience more encouragement, vision, talent, and productivity than when they were operating independently. In fact, they even produced more people!

Third, people who are married well eventually trigger each other's deeper emotional issues, the ones that might never be addressed otherwise, like shame or fear of rejection. Need I mention, Chuck and Lisa? Getting triggered in this way, though unpleasant, often comes with an opportunity to grow and mature further than if not.

Fourth is pleasure. Usually and naturally, pleasure is the central focus at the beginning of a relationship. Ironically, for pleasure to remain at a high level in a marriage, it must be protected by making it the fourth priority rather than the first. Marital pleasure is safeguarded best when we are being realistic about how we were made, when we are contributing our mutual talents to benefit each other, and when we are willing to grow with conflict.

A best-case marriage is also possible when both parties do these things with a sacrificial commitment to each other's welfare.

Hopefully, this small book will help open a big door of discovery for how truly great your marriage can be, or, in other words, how much relationship you can have with each other. By eliminating your most common enemy, senseless arguing, the path will be clearer.

ABOUT THE AUTHOR

Bill Seery is a Licensed Marriage and Family Therapist. He holds master's degrees in both counseling and theology and has been in private practice for over thirty years. In addition to inpatient and outpatient clinical work, he has done organizational consulting for schools and churches. Bill has also designed in-school programs for teens at risk, produced a video and online tool for parents, and he has written an action-adventure novel called *Above the Summit.* Bill currently conducts a therapy practice in Tucson, Arizona, where he lives with his wife and family.
He has a broad range of interests.

www.ingramcontent.com/pod-product-compliance
Lightning Source LLC
LaVergne TN
LVHW022324200926
848481LV00004B/1417